ALSO BY JOHN MCCULLOUGH

POETRY

Reckless Paper Birds (Penned in the Margins, 2019)
Spacecraft (Penned in the Margins, 2016)
The Frost Fairs (Salt Publishing, 2011)

Panic Response

JOHN MCCULLOUGH

Penned in the Margins
LONDON

PUBLISHED BY PENNED IN THE MARGINS
Toynbee Studios, 28 Commercial Street, London E1 6AB
www.pennedinthemargins.co.uk

All rights reserved
© John McCullough 2022

The right of John McCullough to be identified as the author of this work has been asserted by him in accordance with Section 77 of the Copyright, Designs and Patent Act 1988.

This book is in copyright. Subject to statutory exception and to provisions of relevant collective licensing agreements, no reproduction of any part may take place without the written permission of Penned in the Margins.

First published 2022

Printed in the United Kingdom by TJ Books

ISBN
978-1-913850-05-0

This book is sold subject to the condition that it shall not, by way of trade or otherwise, be lent, re-sold, hired out, or otherwise circulated without the publisher's prior consent in any form of binding or cover other than that in which it is published and without a similar condition including this condition being imposed on the subsequent purchaser.

CONTENTS

Glass Men	11
J	13
Electric Blue	16
Quantum	17
Candyman	19
Letter to Lee Harwood	22
Prayer for a Godless City	24
Pour	26
Mantle	28
A Chronicle of English Panic	30
,	32
And Leave to Dry	33
Scoundrel	35
Error Garden	36
Invisible Repairs	38
Flower of Sulphur	39
Coombeland Mannequin	43
Worms	45
Scrambled Eggs	47
Oops, I Did It Again	50
Self-Portrait as a Flashing Neon Sign	52

&	53
Inside Edward Carpenter	55
Old Ocean's Bauble	57
Bungaroosh	58
Six!	60
Mr Jelly	62
Crown Shyness	64
ACKNOWLEDGEMENTS	69
NOTES	71

for Morgan and my parents

Panic Response

Glass Men

Brain tissue inside a man's skull at Pompeii had turned to glass through heat.

When my head is molten, I hide with ice packs near an electric fan.

A therapist suggests my overworking began as a way to please a disappointed father.

Charles VI of France believed he was made of glass.

I have no wish to blame my father, who has his own private volcano.

When glass fractures, the cracks leap faster than 3,000 miles an hour.

My father's running medals hibernate in boxes on a shelf.

In fight-or-flight mode, blood gushes to muscles, hyperventilation flaps its shadow.

My body prepares to race north to the Arctic, across the sea.

The smartphone may be said to function as an apex predator.

No shelter withstands repeated storms of ash.

Laying the predator facedown will not save anyone.

To build a short-term haven, I inhale slowly, sweeping arms above my head.

At my best, I end text messages to Dad *love John*.

Small refuges with walls of air can, on occasion, seem enough.

I write this while my hands are shaking.

J

And so it starts, though I cannot.
Despite my being unable to say the first words
there is a voice doing it, this not-speaking.

There are risks. Even now, Marie Curie's notebooks
are so radioactive no one can hold them.
Likewise, there are phrases that I (whoever this is)
am reluctant to approach, to slide from their lead-lined box
in case my skin candles to green, words I cannot form
without a chance of my teeth falling out.

Books can kill you. I know this.
I read and read and woke one night with a clawed hand
squeezing my brain. I stumbled to the bathroom
past a tower of loans from a library's Renaissance corner.
I had dissected every text, by which I mean I incised
their skins then weighed their organs in my palms,
warm kidneys, spleens and lungs,
till each went cold and I realised I'd been removing
pieces of myself, a little at a time.

My throat closed and the sound wouldn't rise.
No one could get within a hundred miles.
I grasped my phone and all that fell from my lips
were the noises of a failed genetic experiment:
the grunts of a boar, an owl's screech
as it heard its own limits.

I lay curled in an armchair for weeks
staring at my hands, my skin so sheer
I split open at the lightest brush
of sound. I became a vessel of many silences:
the quiet of a locked room, braided
with the nearly-not-there of a tree;
a pause in a quarrel, tongue cropped
with one flick of a wrist.
I had to learn to talk again, practised
for hours shaping *J*, a narrow tunnel
of breath, just to say my name.

Now I can talk, in the basalt of my head
I sense sealed cracks that one day might reopen.
It makes me listen. I follow the quivering tongues
of tulips. The sky withholds its voice

and I linger. It is forming a syllable,
not the bellows of thunder but something else
trying and trying to begin, almost getting there
in this gathering of restless air.

Electric Blue

The radiance is visiting again,
    a bloom of shimmering plankton at low tide
that lifts the brutal shore to space.

Conditions must be perfect for their blue glow,
    the darkness total. They must be far from home,
completely lost, exiled by currents

then panicked by the foamy smack
    of breakers. This is no bounty for them. It's horror,
this brilliance that quivers, arcs.

Picture it now so you'll remember the scene
    one lonely midnight when your heart assaults
your ribs: the galactic light of tiny selves

that never wanted anything like this
    but, together, finished up terrified, magnificent,
brightly living the only way they know.

Quantum

i.m. Avril Brown, 1951-2002

Now and then, the past flutters
out of a cupboard. I cradle a yellowed
newspaper cutting — Mrs Brown,
my chemistry teacher, found dead.
~~Her husband stabbed her forty-seven times~~
~~with a screwdriver. He barely spoke~~
~~a civil word to her, said the prosecutor,~~
~~once he lost his job after a stroke~~
~~while she became Head of Department.~~

This needs correcting. Avril was a lilac
potassium flame. She talked to phosphorus,
encouraged it to turn hexagonal.
Her clan: gauze, tongs, crucible.
She never gave up on experiments,
including the boy who kept smashing
conical flasks, whose thermometers
rolled off desks to their doom.
Oh, for goodness' sake. Here: try again.

In the picture that comes when I hear
her name, she is tilting, arms spread,
as she tears around the lab, apeing
an excited electron — how it radiates
vigour, shapes light. You cannot kill
an electron. It has no substructure.

Avril, in this image, is both particle
and wave, past and future, her grin wide
as she accelerates, decade after decade.

Candyman

For three centuries, *worrying* described mainly how a wolf
    mauls its prey's throat.

Now I'm the one with giant teeth.

I stalk myself, ravenous, pounce wherever meat's exposed.

Mostly I long to be understood, for others to know why I act
    this way, but what if *I* don't understand either?

Wittgenstein thought the word *I* oversimplified, led to falsely
    neat descriptions.

Each self is a plural place.

The past is cloudy today, swells close to ceilings before it falls
    as sticky rain.

In a council estate in Watford, 1995, a frothy island of spit
    on a paving slab stares back.

Best walk quickly, poof, I've got a knife.

Each time we glimpse a memory, our brains adjust it slightly.

When I return to Watford, roads from twenty-five years ago don't exist nor any boys who spat.

An army of TV aerials judders; a vine with pale pink blossom sways.

Knowing a living thing's name stops you seeing the individual clearly — you say *honeysuckle* instead of *hello*.

Without their indistinctness things do not exist; you cannot desire them (Elizabeth Bowen, *The House in Paris*).

Blurs and shadows make a face alive, create the tenderness of one specific neck.

I am almost convinces more than *I am*.

A gecko's shed skin looks unearthly but is still, for the gecko, a handy snack.

I gaze at a ceiling where the residue of a storm diffuses.

Tonight I do not need to be understood.

I hanker only for candy floss, to bite into cloud, feel a phantom dissolve on my tongue.

Letter to Lee Harwood

> *if snow fell upwards*
>   TRISTAN TZARA, 'the death of guillaume apollinaire', trans. L.H.

Dear Lee, forgive me. I need your gentleness.
The world stinks of panic — trapped heat; taller seas;

bleached coral, its skeletons exposed.
A virus keeps half my friends off the streets.

They ghost beside shut windows. Loneliness
is a turbulent factory. It makes things no one wants.

My elderly neighbour says his tap water's dodgy.
Really cloudy now. A sort of chloride taste.

He's petrified of envelopes: touching paper
then his lips, both hands chapped from scrubbing.

The golems in charge could not name our dead nurses
or bus drivers but are *very proud* of the government response

and we should all try our best to *move on*.

Those are the words for their new national anthem

but England keeps smoking its people, dropping bodies
on concrete, stamping the rubber heel of its boot.

You're right, I know: the past wasn't golden.
It wasn't even ormolu. History is the armchair

by the kerb that says TAKE ME I'M FREE!
but is too heavy to carry. Still, walking into the city,

I keep imagining one face behind a mask will be you
and you'll tug it down, tell me softly how you're not

really dead, how tender minutes might show up,
make all this infected snow fall up into sky.

Prayer for a Godless City

Air, on earth as you are in heaven, please nurse
our converted churches. Granite gargoyles
cling on over hipster offices. Our angel statue is trapped
in hallucination, its back turned to rapacious sea.

The pews here are benches for the frayed and sundered
who believe in nothing they cannot clutch or smell
like warm dogs, Frosty Jack's, gnawed chicken legs
forsaken in doorways where death whispers.

Bless us, air, we who linger, exposed to wide open space
where you lunge after roaming the Atlantic
with your cargo of salt, dust and recycled breath,
unbalancing the crowns of elms not far from shore.

Keep slamming into our faces, coursing down
the windpipes of stoners who kite hazily above their legs,
who kneel in bushes on cruising grounds
while you give yourself without judgment

to council estates where the glows of lone cigarettes
at night are souls drifting; to each corner beneath bridges
where trolleys congregate, buskers cry; to the flat
where a woman rises from under bathwater, gasping.

Pour

Coleridge said readers fall into four categories —
sandglasses, sponges, strain-bags and Mogul diamonds —
the lowest being sandglasses who *retain nothing*,
though he deemed sodomy *that very worst of all
possible vices* and my lecturer who cried
reading out 'Frost at Midnight' agreed that sexual
reproduction was *the true meaning of life*
so other meanings we discover are false and blur
the picture and every time I clean the bathroom I make
a cloth grubby and now and then I fall into myself
and no one can reach me and it's certainly fair
to say I can't remember why I'm here and have no sense
of what the cosmos might be up to, though a vacuum,
I've heard, is not a lifeless nothing but a blizzard
of subatomic events and almost anything could happen there —
for instance, though it's very unlikely, a queer bar
could suddenly appear and maybe the universe itself
began as a spontaneous quirk in absence and so many
of our most terrible fears are imaginary —

you cannot drown in quicksand and the orange snow
that fell on Sochi in 2018 wasn't toxic, being simply
Siberian flurries that crashed into sand-filled wind
from the Sahara, a desert on the move, which makes me
picture my friends who moved to this city and what
they're up to in this moment — fucking and washing up
and snorting K, listening to podcasts or deep house
and passing each other in the street, eyes meeting briefly
before one's diverted by a hot splash of orange tulips
in a bucket outside the station that surely can't last
though such souls belong in this city of sandglasses
and I'm happy to let them and everything else
pour through me till my head is completely empty —

Mantle

a low tumble of bells
the wall with a veil

        and I'm there
        of water descending

my fingertip dividing it
we inhabited

        into wings as it fell.
        a landscape of silence

a tundra
hotel slippers

        of small words unspoken
        like shocked mice

their slap
I left in adamant rain

        on each marble stair.
        for anywhere else

the torrent piercing
drenching my copy

        my rucksack
        of Mansfield's letters.

how strange talking is
losing and finding

        she writes
        a presence

then down comes another
the last time we spoke

        soft final curtain.
        I explained

| to a phone how nerves | had me bedbound. |
| *yes of course* | you murmured |

| and I sensed again | the first drops |
| how I'd keep being there | leaving the hotel |

| with what little I'd brought | holding overhead |
| a soaking map | against the years. |

A Chronicle of English Panic

1900 Arthur Conan Doyle catches fire at Lord's when a cricket ball clouts the matchbox in his pocket.

1909 A field mouse dodges between the spinning wheels of three carriages, vanishes under a door.

1918 Dr Yealland stubs out cigarettes on an ex-soldier's tongue, applies electric shocks to the back of his throat. *And still the coward clings to his disease of manhood.*

1932 On a crowded train platform, two maids in dancing heels on their night off clack along the edge.

1945 The bank clerk stays under his sheets, iron teeth champing, the rowdy sailor who shared his bed gone for good.

1953 Grandmother counts in the living room, awaiting the cuckoo clock's trill or the four-minute warning.

1965 A cockroach scrapes against a policeman's boot,
hurtles away to wash.

1987 At the rumour of thunder, the pensioner who served
with the German army pulls up the zip of his tent
still positioned by the ring road.

1999 A literature professor looks herself up on the
net, finds a woman in Texas with the same name
poisoned a family with cyanide.

2002 Every plane the intern sees makes him feel all sizzle,
skitter, tentacle.

2020 A jogger in Hove distractedly presses a crossing
button, detonates into sweat.

2022 Shark skin under an electron microscope shows
pointed scales: a street covered in flexing spikes.
Behind the big teeth always, the little teeth.

,

There are mail-clad reasons to link sentences with commas, it works well for battle scenes and fluid thinking, though other times it misfires, like when a detail could be poignant but the reader's cannoned through too fast to feel anything but motion sickness, I used to want to see it happen less often, I spread the story that Sophocles died wheezing after performing a soliloquy written without pauses, this year I saw things differently, my mind careered through fields of future catastrophes, they sprang up around me, being sacked, bankruptcy, moving back to where queers get dog shit through the door, all the crises my failure would breed for other people, my role in their looming declines, I'd do anything not to be castled with my thoughts, could bear only the shortest intermissions, I still agree with my former self that if no one's swinging a broken bottle then anxiety mostly needs a full stop so measured breathing can start, there are times now, however, when I'm willing to grant a comma to anybody who needs one,

And Leave to Dry

On Halloween, I'll get my face tattooed blue-grey
and dye my hair white like a photographic negative.
I want to cancel myself. The burglar alarm
inside me's been going off for forty years. I can't stop
stealing from my former selves, telling adventurous lies.
I'd rather be reachable than clever. I carry around
a suitcase filled with spiky voices, a *Who's Who
in Barbed Wire*, and they scare me shitless.
Some Victorians kept hedgehogs in their kitchens
to deal with cockroaches but what did they keep
to deal with hedgehogs? Personally, I'll do anything
to avoid watching predators on wildlife documentaries.
I'd rather eat my own foot. Not that it deserves it.
Please blame the nefarious sponge that's called
my brain. The small tentacles which are my toes
and fingers should receive a lesser sentence, only did
what they were told. Yes, it was me all along
with the spanner in the ballroom. Ever since, I've lived
a new life as a squeaky bone for my personal Cerberus.

I can't stop washing containers, thinking how the handles
of upturned saucepans are long, Pinocchio noses.
I wipe them clean, place every head securely on the rack.

Scoundrel

This week I am theatrical and evil, like a printer.

The revised editions of me churned out are full of typos and beetle larvae, silverfish nibbling the ink.

There is a squid that uses glowing cells to erase its shadow. I keep nurturing mine, setting up its own email and Instagram accounts.

The kitchen vent by my front door pumps out steam so I exit through a fog of wrong.

You really ought to do something about me.

I've tried shutting myself down but always seem to switch on again at 5 a.m., greedy to start chomping your optimism and paper angels, spitting out ghosts.

Error Garden

In Shinjuku, the vending machines are angels.
They flare beside shut salons and noodle bars, confronting
the night, slicing paths through September's sticky heat.
I need all the help I can get. Striding down backstreets,
I blunder round my head. A German word for *maze* captures it:
irrgarten, error garden.
                        Thinking is always chasing,
the mind approaches then loses impossible quarries —
a sequence of stumbling phrases, grasping air.

We left England after my hunts had grown dangerous,
a fretful slamming into walls, faster and harder, heart crashing,
snatching at breath.
                   In Shinjuku, other barriers interrupt me
though already this is exoticized. Say it: walls of heat, walls of rain.

Clear umbrellas are popular. People stare up at what's falling
relentlessly toward them. One manga ad portrays kasa-obake,
umbrella spirits with single eyes and long tongues
that bounce on one leg.

Words are the same. First, they offer shelter,
then they spring out at 4 a.m., won't stop opening, closing.

Edward de Bono says most errors in thinking are *inadequacies
of perception* not logic, but some failures of discernment

are beautiful. In Hama-rikyū Gardens, you strolled around
with a soul on your cap, a black butterfly with a row
of fluorescent blue panels on each wing, slipping
into turquoise near the tips...

The latest wall of rain's ploughed off so I drape my jacket
over one arm, a tired phantom.
                                It's tough to stay vaporous
when each day, you present windows on my life.
When I gaze through, shapes clarify, colours deepen.

Time to return to our hotel where you lie curled in your
    dressing gown.
Time to exchange words and atoms by the yellow blaze
of the vending machine that hovers outside our room,

your fingertips skimming slowly along my neck like a butterfly
that pauses to taste promising ground.

Invisible Repairs

When I come back from the dead,
I visit the boatyard. Men in boiler suits
and goggles purge osmosis blisters,
spray the keels of new, hoisted arrivals.
A smell of turpentine and rubber
beneath unyielding sun.

Further off, though, old boats linger —
loose cleats, splintered gunwales,
the gape of ancient impact damage.
A contest to be the most outrageously
decayed, some here so long
tall weeds cluster inside them.

If you listen, you can hear hulls chatter —

*There's never a bad time
for singing softly.*

*Don't worry. I remember
how I felt on my first day.*

Flower of Sulphur

X   I love poetry but I love my friends more.

C   *In frendship the absent be present, the nedie never lacke, the sicke thyncke them selves whole, and that which is hardest to be spoken, the dead never dye* (Cicero, *De Amicitia*, trans. John Harington, 1550).

S   Friends were my twenties. Stuck for a PhD topic, I stayed inside a known city.

R   *Much that seems effusive to the new scholar is routine. Special and divine friends abound* (John McCullough, *Disputable Friends: Rhetoric and Amicitia in English Renaissance Writing, 1579-1625*, 2005).

T   You were the first friend to take a poetry course of mine. I thought, *This will be a test for me.*

W   *Take an object from the bag and write about its weight and texture.*

P The humanist education system encouraged the keeping of commonplace books with strewn phrases, proverbs on friendship.

A There are twenty-six objects, each linked to a letter of the alphabet. Who has A — the agate?

F Lately, I've been stroking the limits of what I know, what I've forgotten; where this bleeds into what I've never understood.

B Francis Bacon compares friendship to the most painful remedies: Sarza *to open the* Liver; Steele *to open the* Spleene; Flower *of* Sulphur *for the* Lungs (Bacon, 'Of Friendship', *Essayes*, 1625).

M The Bag of Mysterious Objects is sorry. The course I taught you did not save your life.

Y *Al thynges*, Laelius notes, *be by freendship kept togither, and by debate skattered: and this all menne bothe perceive, and prove in very deed* (Cicero, trans. Harington).

N   They found you in the bath, wrists opened. No note.

L   *There is no life without freendeshippe* (Ibid.).

J   You'd started learning Japanese. You were heading for Wakayama Prefecture in six months' time. No one knows what you planned to do there.

E   Laelius calls the prolonged mourning of a friend an error. *For a man to be grevously troubled for his owne losses, it is selfly love, and not frendly love* (Ibid.).

Q   I didn't go to your funeral. Why, I don't know. Whether this was wrong or right, I don't know.

H   Unable to write one PhD chapter, I had a breakdown, moved back in with my parents.

U   For five days after you died, it snowed and snowed. I built a white cat in my front garden, sticks for arms.

G   *He that beholdeth his friend, doeth as it wer behold a certain patterne of him selfe* (Ibid.).

D The snowcat's arms dropped away in the night.

Z In Wakayama, there is a shrine that has a yearly service for broken sewing needles that worked hard and now rest in a soft bed of tofu.

K The signs of friendship do not mean as fully or securely as is expected of an ideal to be preferred *beefore all kynde of worldely thynges* (Ibid.).

V After my viva, I lost all interest in Renaissance friends. I use my PhD as a doorstop.

I Still, I stroke the gaps.

O *The order of the alphabet is arbitrary,* you said. *Why not start at X?*

Coombeland Mannequin

Beyond the council estate, there is only the vastness of fields. Knuckles of flint, a chalk ridge lying flat as a femur, and me striding with a headless mannequin.

Wait up, you used to say. No need to be that jockey who won the race despite being dead. *Look around!*

Today: a pylon that's already forgotten why it wandered out here, that's soon to meet a mannequin named Dennis. There is a closed Facebook group called Dennis Can't Find A Head. I stop and photograph him leaning against the torsos of rusted wrecks, cars joy-ridden from the estate, ditched on coombeland. Bonnets flung up, steel innards scattered — a bomb site.

You set up the group. You liked the farce of it. Dennis at the boatyard by museum-glass water, red crates washed out to pink. Dennis in a recycling bin, legs projecting at 45 degrees. Dennis by penny falls on the pier, brown coins nudged into the mass, disappearing.

It horrified you, the idea of staying in one place, ghost stuck in a moment. You found heads for Dennis but each confined him. This one was too beautiful. This one, too sad. That one had a blue stain beneath its nose. *I literally can't go on like this any longer.*

What you did to yourself at last, when you could take no more of your brain scorching, ensured you would not be any kind of mannequin.

I lay Dennis on his side, rest my camera. I scratch a wavy line in chalk beside him, cover my hands in white dust. It makes me almost happy, a vague thickening like spun sugar: a good minute, unfathomable. Is that all happiness is? An absence, no lingering crow in the rear-view mirror?

I don't want to be a mannequin so I look at power lines overhead — lines for the living. I dream of setting out over coombeland in mist, the tops of pylons poking through, and voicing a spell that saves them somehow — everyone in my life beyond rescue — as if anything so fractured as language might help, as if one human figure could hold back winter.

Worms

If the hotels of Regency Square are crying
    after rain, it's only self-pity. Each pretends
the others don't exist, just as most never think

about the giant car park secreted under grass,
    lone Corsas that slink away at dawn.
Locals try to forget the slender young junkie

who crammed his belly with buttercups,
    died of multiple organ failure a pebble's throw
from where Oscar and Bosie were shaken like dice

when their horse-drawn carriage smashed
    into railings. *An accident of no importance.*
Why, then, does the moment keep replaying

in my mind today, walking home
    on Holy Wednesday? After Oscar died,
the disownment. Lord Douglas stumbled

through marriage and prison then returned,
    took refuge streets from here. He avoided sun,
tunnelled into memory to document his youth.

Did he watch the crash repeat, feel their torsos
    collide, long fingers twisting down Oscar's back
before they climbed out and stood apart

on the spot where needles still slide into veins,
    where a seagull's outlandish dance never fails
to bring worms to the surface?

Scrambled Eggs

Panic, from the Greek god Pan, unexplained sounds in a forest. I hunker down in my cup of branches —

Last night, I became trapped between the walls of 4 a.m.

A crowd bunches beneath the shower head. I'm joined in the sizzle of water by my least favourite teacher, two priests, a mugger. I soap and sponge but no one leaves —

Death sits on the work surface, teeth chattering while I make scrambled eggs. Long eyelashes. A bit like Justin Bieber.

At a subatomic level, no two bodies quite join. You're Monday, I'm Wednesday. We never really touch. Secretly, though, we were never really separate.

Anxiety is a frilly word, too trifling. Sonically, its texture's light and bland. The *x* is its only interesting feature, marks the tender spot —

Memories of the streets of Watford give me goosebumps, each forearm suddenly a sci-fi city of domes. The recently dead get goosebumps too. What are they afraid of, coming back?

So often, what I don't know is more important than what I do. If rescue arrives it's from an unexpected angle — a different dimension, a trapdoor beneath my feet or in the sky.

This morning, I am a portrait in Elizabethan colours: dead Spaniard, ape's laugh, milk-and-water. I should have disappeared centuries back.

I can only show you pieces of me — flotsam bobbing on uncertain currents. Health and safety nightmare. I understand how scary it must be to leap aboard.

One January, I saw Christmas trees torn apart and gobbled by giraffes at a zoo. The end of my joy is frequently someone else's feast, and don't they, too, deserve happiness?

Unable to sleep, I listen at my bedroom window to the storm, find accumulations of sound like countries — Australias of rain on a tin roof; plothering Americas; Englands with a thousand, tiny hammers.

I crave the tidiness of a palpable full stop, like when the ashes of the inventor of the Pringles can were buried in a Pringles can. The snug fit of that lid, the little puff of air —

At the greengrocer's, a pile of dreaming turnips are eyeballs. They stared into the dark for months, never imagining light existed till the sun caught their tops, purpled them.

When a drop hits the puddle, the upside-down hotel dissolves relentlessly then relentlessly reforms.

Today I'm not fully present in conversation, a book shelved back to front. Still available to the curious, I require persistence, a forgiving hand —

I'm a flight to New York where a baby screeches and a voice from the back yells *Shut up!* I'm the pilot, the thin man wanking in the toilet, the hopeful steward wiping sick, delivering pillows.

Oops, I Did It Again

Error, from the Latin *errare*, to stray — a deviation
        from correctness. I spell my surname wrong
    on the estate agent's form or assume the atlas moth
roofing my hand is a finch. Browning used *twat*
       in 'Pippa Passes', thinking it was what a nun
    wore on her head. The great American poet
      I sent my work to felt one last line was *a leap too far* —
the undeleted instruction *SORT OUT*
    THIS FUCKING AWFUL ENDING.
I don't think I ever did. My dodgy sat-nav always sends me off
    the highway too early, too late.
               The one question:
what colour is my catastrophe today?
          That email to a straight male editor with a string
of kisses: claret. My doomed relationship with Craig:
    dark blue. In the nineteenth century, there were manifold
    sightings of a nonexistent planet called Vulcan.
It hangs over me still, guiding experiments
    which seem like failures only for a while.

Ripped apart by error,
I wake up naked, the filthy air remembering everything,
   even the dream where, after I spilled tea
      on Noël Coward's shirt cuff, he whispered
         How alive of you.
            Go on: do it again.

Self-Portrait as a Flashing Neon Sign

My green face is enormous on the hill.
The night sky is assaulted
by my ridiculous nose,
a skew-whiff cap and ionized grin.

I am a jumble of lightning bottled
in the loop and swerve of glass,
Watford-lairy, off my trolley —
bumped off then resurrected, time and again.

I pound the retinas of innocent pedestrians,
spark petitions. I am too much.
Boys canoodle under my chin, uneducated
by the empty clarity of my presence.

I smile on, assist dog walkers, mystify drunks.
I am a fizz in their cytoplasm.
I am frying the dark.
I am lucky as a ninety-nine-leafed clover.

&

i.m. John Ashbery, 1927-2017

How much beauty would you like with your pond today? Monet paid a gardener to dust his waterlilies before he painted them, messed their petals up the right way.

It's always a problem. The shimmering ones twirl past your window and you feel like a disused petrol station. Though it's no good waiting beside a cuckoo clock as if you were a stalker. That's just putting the cuckoo in charge.

The harp sponge traps its prey in the beautiful grill of its body. It dissolves small fish, cell by cell. But sponges have no brains. Are they wicked? Sometimes you don't really need to ask, end up saying *ping-pong tree sponge* because you can, so you might spring free from a warehouse of Januaries. You buy colour-changing lights or, at the bakery, a cluster of ampersand-shaped doughnuts: & & &.

How do the beautiful feel about this? I hear the frozen waterfall holds no particular position on being a metaphor for just about everything. Should it be thanked, even though it wouldn't care? *Thank you*, originally from *think*, as in *I will remember what you did for me*. This, despite the impossibility of recalling every beautiful entity you've thanked, especially the trees.

Of course, it's not up to you anyway. The Edwardian houses opposite didn't ask for your permission to exist and neither did their artful arrangement of strangers. You had no say, any more than you did on gravity or being born, the century and timeline your flesh popped up in, like dubious toast.

Yet it seems more than acceptable to be lost in a new and beautiful manner, the way an eel curling over fenland in its sleeve of mucus can find itself of a sudden in someone's garden, then gobbles up beans and peas.

And this is only the latest chapter, this body that — whatever you do — eventually unwinds, visited increasingly by invisible animals of silence. They float in and out of the living room, gentle as manatees, drifting through on long, beautiful migrations.

Inside Edward Carpenter

> Brunswick Square, 2001

I stop beside the house where you were born,
    my back to miles of ocean, slabs of cloud.

This city was meant to be my bandage,
    Edward, but mostly I spend days oystered

beneath a stinking quilt, wait in bars
    where no one talks. During your decline,

post-Cambridge, you shrank to an icicle,
    a brittle curate till you chanced on *Leaves of Grass*.

You melted, wrote to Walt, enraptured
    by his multitudes, *the large spaces you make*

all round one. You met George, a coarse-fleshed,
    oil-smeared dream, and he kindled your lectures

on spiritual democracy, shared his coat

    amid a blizzard of voices throughout Oscar's trial.

I don't know what I'm travelling toward
    but hope it's not too far from this. May I learn

how slow hands can wake philosophy;
    how, with patience, a man can sail

through Arctic water, stare into the blue fog
    of his body and find a soft battalion.

Old Ocean's Bauble

They scooped it from the Channel:
    an NBA basketball with a thick beard
of goose barnacles, long and smooth.

To gaze at it was to reach and caress it
    underneath, fingers wakening the rich clatter
of shells. It was like stroking knowledge,

the accumulations of a head that had sailed
    inside itself for years, saying nothing, veering
anywhere, spiralled by eddies and gyres.

They knew there was no alternative
    but to put it back, let it take up again
a looping voyage with no destination.

They understood that others could need
    this prophecy, might stare into its eyeless,
mouthless face, construe the terrible warning.

Bungaroosh

In Brunswick Square, the houses refuse your refusal.
There's no ignoring the Regency swell of bay windows,
pilasters the colour of clotted cream.
Light bounces like a mind
                        that's outwitted its own soberness,
that's made a gorgeous thought solid to keep catapulting
the eye back to delight.

                     I just can't see a way out, says Tim in the café.
He clutches gloves in one fist, their grey fingers splayed: a caught squid.
In three days, his husband's left him, the landlord wants him gone
and now he's heading to an interview where he thinks he might cry.
What would you do?
                At the next table, a teenage boy hacks at a scone.
Who am I to reassure given the suspect breathing apparatus
beneath my ribs?
                Last summer, my light got lost inside me.
Total internal reflection, said the physicist on TV once she'd trapped
a laser beam in the waterfall. *Round and round it goes…*

Victorians saw the square's use of stucco fronts as sham, the depravity
of George IV embodied in architecture.
                        Beneath the triumphant surfaces
lurks bungaroosh: a marmalade of broken bricks, cobblestones, flints
set in mortar that liquefies slowly when wet,
                                          begins to creep.
Magnificent façades still collapse without warning, a torrent
of scrollwork, balconies, deceit.

                        Awaiting disaster each minute,
though, starts electric cascades. I tell Tim I don't have the answer
but it won't be this hard for long and his dashing blue suit and slim tie
hand him a big advantage. He smiles
                        and I feel my own grin extend.

It's how I live this autumn, with the knowledge my walls
are pure bungaroosh, may give way but at present shore up
who they can.
    Listen: not everyone needs to be compact. You can exist
as an unsettled structure
                    and wear any precarious face you have.

Six!

Inebriate of Air – am I –
And Debauchee of Dew –
Reeling – thro endless summer days –
From inns of Molten Blue –
    EMILY DICKINSON

During a recent confinement I greatly overslept, which led to me feeling tired all the time, a circular mistake. I spent too long inside not just my bed but my mind which, if it's a habit that affords gladness now and then, prevents deep delight. *Ecstasy* comes from the Greek *ekstasis*, to stand outside the self. To encounter it, I had to leave my thoughts and commune with the endless, not just the vast space above my head but what collapses distinctions of time.

Dickinson could not have seen Indonesia's Kawah Ijen volcano. Owing to high levels of sulphur, it sends out blue lava. This is only visible at night, which is probably just as well. That *from* which begins her stanza's fourth line is important: no one alive can stay perpetually within *inns of Molten Blue*. Only so much can unfold on the lip of a volcano or mid-air. The limited access we have to boundless pleasure is a condition of its existence.

Another condition for delight is disbelief. To be carried away, you must forget at some level any such experience is possible. Standing in the doorway to my house one morning, something like this happened. After weeks indoors, breathing in so much of what I'd exhaled, I readied myself to tackle a walk. Before taking my first step, I drank in a crisp lungful of freshness so unexpected I was taken out of myself and far into sky. In that moment I, too, became an *Inebriate of Air* — dizzied and staggering, smacked like a cricket ball beyond all thought of days.

Mr Jelly

There is so much I never speak about, more each hour.

I don't celebrate my bones as I can't see them but without them I'd be a pulpy sack.

In 1897, British newspapers feared the telephone would generate unbearable intimacy: *We shall soon be nothing but transparent heaps of jelly...*

Mr Jelly is my favourite Mr Man — fuchsia skin, wavy body.

One website lists his traits as *Wobbly, Uneven, Unbalanced, Inconsistent*, his fears including snapping twigs, sounds from breakfast cereal, gnomes.

Perhaps I should write off what happens inside me as weather but then, with sufficient rain, the side of a mountain slides off —

Freud had a phobia of ferns — rhizome, frond and spore;
the way tight spirals unfurl.

The shape of fronds means ferns unbalance easily, brush
against whatever's near.

What I've still not touched on: like ferns, humans are
luminous — the light's just too weak for primate eyes to see.

Though I can't view anyone's glow, I picture colours as
various as the shades of silence —

thicket green

yolk yellow

wobbling pink

Crown Shyness

for Morgan

Some days I walk the edge of the park
and stop to touch the shrubs. *Dog rose, spindle.*
I smile at everyone I meet, a slow blink

to show I'm no threat. I follow rhythms
of light and sky and the wind that loves me,
that keeps diving into my mouth.

Recently I mislaid my mind again.
I couldn't pour a bowl of cornflakes.
I lay like a zombie beneath a duvet

watching re-runs of *Friends*. The One
Where John Loses It. The One
Where Electricity Cooks John's Head.

The One Where Flying Mountains
Circle Faster And Faster.
My park is called St Ann's Well Gardens.

St Ann was not a saint. She was Annafrieda,
a Saxon whose lover was murdered.
Her tears became an iron-bearing spring

and, later, scented gardens, tennis courts.
Constantinople, my hypnotherapist said in 2003
while I was under. *You will hear that word*

and everything will be OK.
He's dead but I still say the word.
Years after, we honeymooned in Istanbul.

All this is true. Even though you chose
the destination and I never told you my word.
The Blue Mosque, Topkapi Palace, stray cats

that gathered among loose bricks on the shore.
Six weeks ago all I wanted was to stand with you
and gaze up at the green light of leaves,

breathe inside a feline conspiracy.
Conspiracy, from the Latin *conspirare*,
to breathe together. We met here on an early date.

I named the trees: *poplar, sycamore, maple*
and you laughed. I gifted you all
my favourite facts — the five noses of an ant,

how nobody knows who named the Earth.
How the way treetops avoid touching
each other is called *crown shyness*.

You cupped my face and your tongue entered me.
I look at that day from the summit of a stack
of years. So often, perspective transforms all —

from the bottom of a pond, it must seem
as though tadpoles swim through air.
Each mountain returns to dust.

Crown shyness. I love the idea
of a bashful king. Some days I'm the shy monarch
of this park, but so are you. So are our cats

and everything alive. Some days
I meet you here and you bring blue cheese —
which you hate — because I love it.

Some days we walk the edge of the park
together and the green light
of the leaves says *Constantinople*.

ACKNOWLEDGEMENTS

I wish to thank the editors of publications where earlier versions of some of these poems have appeared: *As Above, So Below*; *Envoi*; *Extinction Rebellion: Writers Rebel*; *First Edition: Celebrating 21 Years of Goldsboro Books* (Dome Press, 2020); *The Forward Book of Poetry 2021*; *Impossible Archetype*; *Magma*; *Poetry Birmingham*; *Poetry London*; *The Poetry Review*; *Poetry Wales*; *Queer in Exile*; *Stand*.

I thank also my Hove writing group for their feedback on much of this book: Robert Hamberger, Maria Jastrzębska, Janet Sutherland and Jackie Wills. I've benefitted, too, from the sharp eyes of Gray Behagg, Tom Cowin, Karen Goodwin, Matthew Haigh, Mary J. Oliver, Kate Potts, Jon Stone, Maria Taylor and Alison Winch, plus insights and reading recommendations from Philippa Vafadari.

NOTES

'Candyman'. The quotation from Elizabeth Bowen is from *The House in Paris* (Vintage, 1998), p.118.

'Prayer for a Godless City'. In the Census figures of 2001 and 2011, Brighton and Hove possessed England's largest then second-largest proportion of residents who defined themselves as having 'no religion' (42.4% in 2011).

'Pour'. Coleridge's categories of reader are from the second of his *Lectures on Shakespeare (1811-1819)*, ed. Adam Roberts (Edinburgh University Press, 2016), p.13. His comment on sodomy is part of a marginal annotation concerning Shakespeare's sonnets dated 2nd November 1803. It is in reply to an earlier annotation by Wordsworth in the same volume of Anderson's *British Poets*. Coleridge's annotation is reproduced in its entirety in *Coleridge's Criticism of Shakespeare: A Selection*, ed. R. A. Foakes (Bloomsbury, 1989), pp.30-1.

'Mantle'. The Katherine Mansfield letter cited is addressed to Ottoline Morrell and dated 24th July 1921. It is reproduced in the fourth volume of her *Collected Letters* (Oxford University Press, 1996), p.252.

'A Chronicle of English Panic'. Dr Yealland is Lewis Yealland, the British clinician who authored *Hysterical Disorders of Warfare* (Macmillan, 1918).

'Error Garden'. Edward de Bono's phrase 'inadequacies of perception' appears in *Serious Creativity* (Penguin, 1996), p.58. The butterfly referred to is *Graphium sarpedon nipponum*.

'Worms'. Oscar Wilde's quip was reported in the *Brighton Herald* on 3rd February 1894.

'Old Ocean's Bauble' was written to highlight marine pollution. Its title is a Regency nickname for Brighton coined by the poet Horace Smith, a friend of Shelley.

'Inside Edward Carpenter'. The letter to Walt Whitman quoted here is dated 19th December 1877 and reproduced on whitmanarchive.org.

'Six!' The Emily Dickinson epigraph is taken from the version of 'I taste a liquor never brewed–' in the *Complete Poems* (Faber, 1989), pp.98-9.

'Mr Jelly'. The quotation about telephones is from an anonymous London writer cited in the January 1897 issue of *American Electrician*, and the one about Mr Jelly is from the website mrmen.fandom.com.